Seals

Leo Statts

KAEDEN™
PUBLISHING

Kaeden.com
(800) 890-7323

ISBN: 978-1-63584-118-3

Cover Photo: Maurizio Bonora/iStockphoto, cover
Interior Photos: iStockphoto, 1, 6, 12–13, 19; Ondrej Prosicky/Shutterstock Images, 4–5; Shutterstock Images, 5,
14–15; Stephanie Kuwasaki/iStockphoto, 7; Volodymyr Goinyk/Shutterstock Images, 8; Dmytro Pylypenko/
Shutterstock Images, 9; Ulrike Jordan/Shutterstock Images, 10; Jan Wolffgang/iStockphoto, 11; Red Line Editorial,
13, 20 (left), 20 (right), 21 (left), 21(right); Andrea Leone/iStockphoto, 15; Mark Mowbray/iStockphoto, 16;
Marcos Amend/Shutterstock Images, 17; Vladimir Melnik/Shutterstock Images, 18

Title: FOCUS ON Animals: Seals
Author: Leo Statts
Editor: Brienna Rossiter
Series Designer: Madeline Berger
Art Direction: Dorothy Toth

Printed in Guangzhou, China
NOR/0817/CA21700984

First edition: 2018

Table of Contents

Seals

Seals are related to
sea lions and walruses.
But they are not the same.

Seals do not have ears.
Their front **limbs** are short.

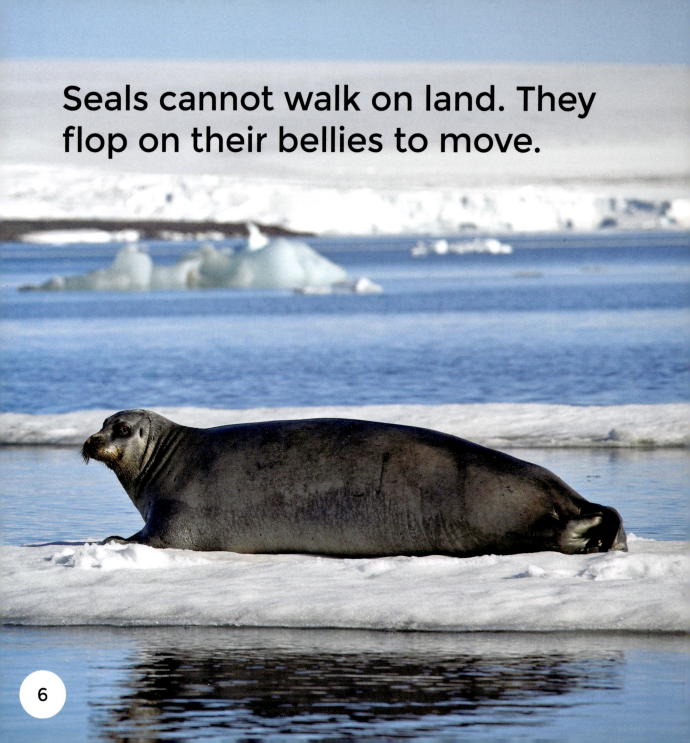

Seals cannot walk on land. They flop on their bellies to move.

But they are great
swimmers and divers.

Body

Seals can be many colors and sizes. They have round middles.

They have small **muzzles**.
Their back **flippers** are large.

Seals have short fur. It covers a layer of **blubber**.

The blubber keeps them warm.
It also helps them float.

Habitat

Seals mainly live in polar areas. They can be found near cold seas. They spend time on land and in the water.

 Where seals live

Seals have trouble moving around on land. They are fast in the water.

Some seals dive deep underwater. They can stay under for more than an hour.

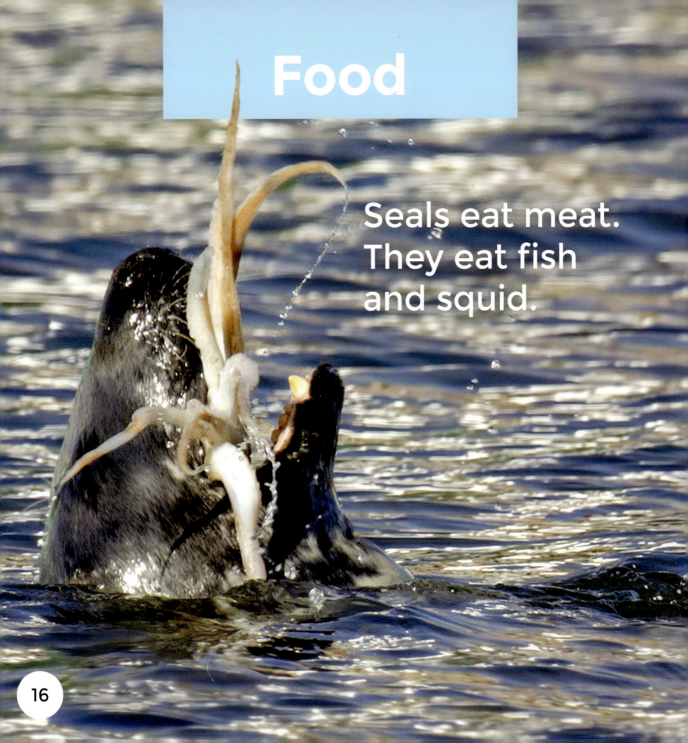

Food

Seals eat meat. They eat fish and squid.

They eat **crustaceans**. Some eat penguins and smaller seals.

Life Cycle

A female seal is called a cow.
A cow has one pup per year.

The pup is born on land. Most seals live approximately 20 years.

Longest Length

A Southern elephant seal is almost as long as a midsize car.

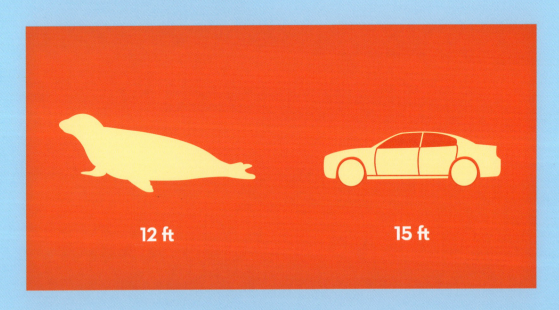

12 ft   15 ft

Quick Stats

Shortest Length

A Baikal seal is a little longer than an acoustic guitar.

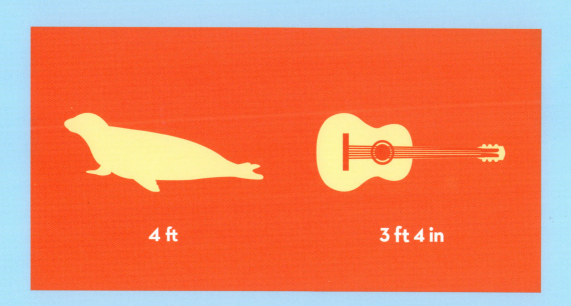

4 ft   3 ft 4 in

Glossary

blubber – fat on marine animals that protects them from the cold

crustacean – any of a group of animals with hard shells that live mostly in water

flippers – wide, flat limbs sea creatures use for swimming

limbs – body parts that stick out, such as arms, legs, or wings

muzzle – an animal's nose and jaw

Index

BOOKS IN THIS SERIES